Love & LIMITS

Elizabeth Crary

GUIDANCE TOOLS *for* CREATIVE PARENTING

A STAR Parenting™ Book

Parenting Press, Inc.
Seattle, Washington

Contents

Cover illustrations and calligraphy by Karen Anne Pew

Manufactured in the United States of America

Library of Congress Cataloguing-in-Publication Data

Crary, Elizabeth, 1942–
  Love & limits : guidance tools for creative parenting/
by Elizabeth Crary. — 1st ed.
    p. cm.
  ISBN 1-884734-05-7 (lib.) — ISBN 1-884734-04-9 (pbk.)
  1. Discipline of children. 2. Child rearing. I. Title.
II. Title: Love and limits.
HQ770.4.C75 1994
649'.64—dc20   93-49556
                                                  CIP

Before You Begin

Everyone Is Different

Parenting is the most wonderful job you can do *and* probably the most frustrating. Successful parenting causes people to grow and change. Parents are pushed and tested in ways unmatched in any other work. I'm glad you're reading this booklet. It suggests that you are willing to grow with your child.

Love & Limits has tools you can use with your children. It has many tools because everyone is different. Something that works well for another person may not work for you. That's okay. There are enough ideas here for everyone. Your job is to find a tool that will work—for both you and your child.

Some people want one tool they can use all the time. There are none. No tool works all the time. This is because children grow and change. When a tool no longer works, try another tool. Keep trying until you find one that works for you and your child.

Both you and your child will feel better about each other because you have used tools that build your child's self-esteem instead of tools that hurt or shame him or her.

Where to Start

Love & Limits offers you both child guidance tools and a four-step process for solving problems. If the problem is serious or really bothers you, use the process to guide you. If your problem is not serious, you can experiment with different tools. First, we will review the tools and then the process.

Star Points and Tools

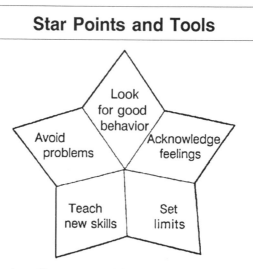

Love & Limits offers many child guidance tools. These tools are grouped into five points or sets of tools. As you can see in the star above, each point focuses on a different aspect of parenting. The more points you use when dealing with a problem, the more likely you will be to resolve the problem satisfactorily.

Avoid the problem. Many problems can be avoided by reducing stress, by changing things or the schedule, or by offering choices. When you reduce the number of hassles with kids you can work more effectively on the issues that are important to you.

Look for good behavior and reward cooperation. The behavior you notice and comment on is the behavior you get. This is true regardless of whether you praise or nag. You can encourage desired behavior by looking for it, giving the child time to cooperate, and rewarding the desired behavior.

Acknowledge feelings. Many problems arise from children's feelings. Children need to know that feelings are different from behavior. And they need to know that their feelings are accepted (not judged or changed). Often, simply acknowledging their feelings reduces objectional behavior.

Set limits. Providing the clear, reasonable rules kids need is an essential skill for effective parenting. There don't have to be many rules, but they need to be clear and reasonable for the child. Back up rules with consequences and dependable follow-through.

Teach new skills. Some parenting conflicts arise because parents expect children to have skills that the children do not have. You can teach new skills (such as sharing, cleaning a room, or managing anger) by modeling, dividing the task into small pieces, and by asking the child to re-do it right.

The three tools for each point of the star are briefly described in the accompanying table.

Summary of points and tools

Star point (tool set)	Purpose of star point (tool set)	Example of tools on that star point
Look for good behavior	To increase good behavior by noticing it	Give attention Praise Reward
Avoid problems	To focus on what is most important	Reduce stress Change things Offer two yeses
Acknowledge feelings	To recognize children's feelings without judging or agreeing	Simple acknowledgment Active listening Grant in fantasy
Set appropriate limits	To establish clear boundaries and let kids test them	Clear rules Reasonable consequences Dependable follow-through
Teach new skills	To offer skills needed for the family and world	Modeling Shaping Re-do it right

Problem-Solving Process

Love & Limits offers a simple problem-solving process. It is easy to remember and easy to use. It is based on the word STAR. Each letter stands for one step in the process:
  S — Stop and focus
  T — Think of ideas
  A — Act effectively
  R — Review, revise, reward

   Stop and focus on yourself, your child, and the problem. Get an idea of where you are and where you want to go before you do something that may make life more difficult for you and your child.
   Think of ideas. Lots of ideas. Different ideas. You can use the star tools (described in the next section) as a place to start.
   Act effectively. The most wonderful plan will not work if you don't "do it." Pick your battles. Chose your timing. Get the support you need to carry out the plan.
   Review, revise, reward. Few plans work completely the first time. Most successful parents need to tweak their plans several times before the situation is satisfactorily resolved. Reward yourself for effort or success.

Commitment

Tools and a plan will only be successful if you know what you want. Otherwise, the day-to-day frustrations and pressures will tempt you to make decisions that will work against you in the long run. Take time to look at what you want for your child.

Understanding Kids
What's reasonable, what's not.

It is easier to guide children's behavior when your expectations are realistic. Children differ both in development and temperament. Often well-meaning parents confuse normal developmental behavior with defiance or irresponsibility.

Developmental Tasks

Age	Children's Tasks	Parents' Tasks
0-6 months	**Being:** To decide to grow and trust.	• Nurture, love, care for, and support babies.
6-18 months	**Exploring:** To explore their world.	• Provide a safe environment for toddlers to explore.
18-36 months	**Thinking & feeling:** To begin to think. To distinguish between thinking and feeling. To separate from their parents.	• Encourage thinking. • Distinguish between feelings and behavior. • Accept children's feelings. • Recognize "No's" as the beginning of separation rather than as disobedience.
3-6 years	**Power & identity:** To observe how people (both men and women) get what they want. To decide how to use power.	• Model appropriate use of power. • Establish consequences for misuse of power. • Accept children's need to test limits without feeling personally threatened.
6-12 years	**Structure:** To find out how the world works. To develop a structure for living in it.	• Offer children skills and support as they develop rules for living with their peers and family. • Help children make decisions and motivate *themselves* to follow through.

Temperament

Researchers found nine personality traits that are relatively constant through time. People can be intense on one trait and low on another. Most people fall between the extremes. Each trait is valuable in some situations and a handicap in others.

Traits that often distress parents are high activity, high intensity, and high persistence. If you have an active, intense, persistent child, your life with him or her will be more challenging than if your child is quiet. However, the same traits that are frustrating in children are wonderful in adults. The challenge is learning how to work with them.

Temperament Traits

Activity level—some kids have high activity and energy levels, while others have low energy and rarely fidget.

Intensity—some children are intense whether they are happy or mad. Others are quiet and reserved most of the time.

Approach/withdrawal—some kids automatically approach new people, food, or situations. Others initially resist most new things.

Adaptability—some children adapt quickly to change regardless of their initial opinion. Other children take weeks or months to adapt.

Sensitivity to physical world—Some children are extremely aware of light, sound, temperature, and texture of clothes and things. Others are oblivious to the physical world.

Mood—some children are born happy and cheerful. Others are often irritable and upset.

Persistence—some children have a long attention span, even for things they have difficulty with. Others have a short attention span.

Regularity—some children have a precise internal clock. They eat, sleep, and toilet at the same time each day. Other children have an irregular clock. They nap hours one day and 15 minutes another.

Distractibility—some children are easily distracted by activities going on around them. Other children are rarely distracted by people, noise, or activity.

Look for
Good Behavior
First set of tools

The easiest way to get good behavior is to look for it.

When you find good behavior:

- Pay attention to it.
- Praise it.
- Reward it.

People see what they expect to see. If you expect kids to be bad, you will see more bad behavior than good behavior. And if you expect them to be good, you will see good behavior.

Give Attention

All children need attention.

If they can't get attention by acting good, they will act bad.

Strangely, children do what parents notice. If you notice your children being good, they are more likely to be good. If you notice them acting "bad," they are more likely to misbehave.

Many parents have trouble seeing good behavior. Sometimes that is because there isn't much good behavior to see. More often it is because parents aren't used to looking for it.

Five ways to help you notice more good behavior are:

✓ List ten things you would like your child to do. Spend three minutes each hour looking for those things. Each time your child does something on the list, put a check by the item.

✓ Ask someone to help you look. Work together. See how long a list you can make in ten minutes. Try again an hour later.

✓ Reward *yourself* when you notice something good. (More about rewards later.)

✓ Ask your child's teacher or daycare provider to tell you three positive traits or behaviors of your child. Look for those behaviors.

✓ Spend five minutes three times each day looking for good behavior. Put a star or check mark on a calendar each time you notice some good behavior.

When you see your kids acting pleasant—give them attention. Let your children know you liked their behavor.

✓ Smile at them.

✓ Sit down beside your child and give him a hug.

✓ Praise them. Say, *"Thank you for walking quietly."*

The more good behavior you notice, the more good behavior you will get.

Praise

Praise can help or make things worse.

Three guides for helpful praise are: Be specific. Be sincere. Be immediate.

Specific praise tells your child exactly what she did right. Specific praise is simple, not exaggerated. It focuses on the *behavior,* not the person.

General (or personality) praise doesn't tell your child what you like. For example, if you say *"Good girl, Molly,"* she doesn't know what to do again—close the front door, hang up her coat, sing a song, or walk quietly. Sometimes children guess right, sometimes they don't. *"Good girl"* can change to *"I'm pleased you hung up your coat."*

Exaggerated praise can set up unreasonable expectations. Children either believe they are the greatest, or they don't believe the praise at all. *"You are the best painter"* can become *"I like your picture."*

Sincere praise feels true. Somehow children know whether people are telling the truth or not.

If you say, *"That is a beautiful picture,"* but really think the picture is awful, children know something is wrong. If you want to say something nice, find a part of the picture you like. For example, *"I like the colors you used,"* *"This is an interesting shape,"* or *"You look like you enjoyed drawing."*

Immediate praise gives information while children *still remember* what they did.

Young children need information right away. With babies and toddlers praise should be immediate. If you wait, it probably won't work.

Here are ten examples you can adapt:

Thank you—for helping put away the toys.

Well done!— You put away all the blocks.

I like the way—you touched me gently.

Terrific— you got your coat on by yourself.

Wow—you found a good way to say you're mad.

Wonderful— you remembered to sit on the sofa.

Nice work— setting the table.

I'm glad—you remembered to use your spoon.

Excellent— you really came quickly when I called.

I noticed— you used words to ask for a drink.

Praise effort as well as success. For example, *"I like the way you tried to. . . ."*

Once you get used to giving specific praise you won't need to use the starter words.

Reward

Rewards help children learn faster.

A reward needs to be something the *child* wants. The reward needs to be given right away. The reward can be anything. It can be something you give or time you spend together. Different children need different rewards.

Here are twenty ideas. Star the ideas that already work with your child right now. Check which ideas might also work.

☐ stars
☐ stickers
☐ pennies
☐ play money
☐ a smile
☐ crackers
☐ toys
☐ a hug

☐ small cars
☐ time with you
☐ doll clothes
☐ baking cookies
☐ reading a story
☐ sugarless gum
☐ blowing bubbles
☐ trip to library

☐ an ice cream cone
☐ walk around the block
☐ making a cereal necklace
☐ toys from cereal boxes
☐ dinosaur erasers

Give a reward for a specific behavior. Give rewards every time your child does the specific behavior you want. Some people have questions about rewards.

How is a reward different from a bribe?

A reward focuses on good behavior. A bribe focuses on bad behavior. A child gets a reward *after* he has behaved well or finished a task. A bribe is given *ahead of time* to stop misbehavior.

Why reward children for what they should do?

Because it is easier and more fun for everyone.
A reward helps a child learn quicker.

Will I have to keep giving rewards forever?

Fortunately, no.
When your child begins to learn the behavior— gradually reduce the rewards.

Avoid Problems
Second set of tools

The easiest way to solve a problem is to avoid it.

You avoid problems by preventing them, not pretending they don't exist. There are three simple things you can do to avoid problems:

- Make expectations clear ahead of time.
- Give children two *yeses* for each *no*.
- Change the situation.

Make Expectations Clear

Help your children cooperate by telling them specifically what you want or expect from them.

Often parents think a child is rude or difficult when he or she just doesn't understand what the parent wants. Three steps to make your expectations clear are:

1. Get your child's attention,
2. Tell your child what *to do*, and
3. Use clear language.

Get your child's attention. Move close to your child. Kneel or sit down so you are on her level. Look her in the eye or touch her gently on the shoulder. When you have her attention, tell her what you expect.

Tell your child what to do—instead of what *not* to do.
Avoid words like *no, stop,* and *don't*. They are difficult for preschool children to understand. If you say *"no hitting,"* your child may think it is okay to pinch, punch, and poke. If you say *"touch gently,"* what you want is much clearer. Some common changes are:

Stop running becomes **Walk.**
No hitting becomes **Touch gently.**
Don't touch becomes **Look only.**
Don't pee on the rug becomes **Pee in the potty.**
No grabbing becomes **Ask for a turn.**
Stop yelling becomes **Speak softly.**

If you have trouble deciding what you want, your child will have *much more* trouble figuring out what you want.

Use language children understand. Most adults use phrases whose meanings are different from the words in the phrase. For example, *"hold on a minute"* means *"wait a bit,"* not hold on to my arm or wait 60 seconds.

You can avoid a number of problems if you decide what you want your child *to do*, use clear language, and be sure you have your child's attention *before* you speak.

Give Two Yeses for Every No

Tell your child how to succeed, rather than how to fail.

Offer your child two ways to do what he or she wants. For example, if Troy wants to hammer on the window say, *"Troy, you can hammer on the floor or on the cobbler's bench, but not on the window."*

You can find new choices by changing:

- location
- tool
- activity
- time

For example, Josh wants to drink grape juice on the living room rug. You don't want him to because it would stain the rug if he spilled it. He can—
- drink grape juice in the *kitchen,*
- make a popsicle of grape juice and yogurt,

- drink *water* in the living room, or
- drink grape juice in the living room the day before you clean the rug.

Sometimes all the choices are not workable.
Your options may be limited because of safety, time, money, energy, or something else.

For example, Mary wants to throw a hard ball at the window. She can—

- throw the ball *outside,*
- *roll* the ball on the floor instead,
- throw a *pillow or foam ball* at the window, or
- no *time* choice acceptable. A hard ball cannot be thrown at the window safely at any time.

What do you do when offering choices doesn't work? We will discuss that in the chapter on setting appropriate limits.

Change the Situation

Change the situation to avoid problems.

You can change the situation by changing:

- the environment or setting, or
- your child's schedule and activities.

Changing the environment is often the easiest solution if the problem occurs again and again. You can:

- add,
- remove, or
- change things around at home.

For example, Jesse (16 months) sees a glass bowl of fruit on the table and he wants to play with it. You can (1) get out a toy he likes and distract him, (2) put the glass bowl away until he is older, or (3) put a plastic bowl on the table.

You can change time or activities by planning more time, rescheduling things, or doing them in a different order.

There are two times of day that are difficult for many parents—mornings and evenings. Mornings are hard when parents are hurrying to get ready for work or school. The hour before supper when everyone is tired and hungry is also frustrating.

To avoid problems plan to take more time, do some things earlier or later, or on a different day. The following are ways to restructure difficult mornings and evenings:

Mornings
- get up earlier
- wake your child earlier
- set out clothes the night before
- collect everything you will need the night before
- make lunches the night before
- put bowls of cereal on the table the night before

Before supper
- fix supper earlier in the day
- fix several suppers on the weekend and freeze them
- make and eat a snack before starting supper
- find ways to have your child help you fix supper
- play a game with your child before you start supper

If you have trouble thinking of ideas to change the environment, time, or activities, ask other people for ideas. Try not to judge the ideas at first.

Keep asking until you get ten ideas. The ideas should be different, but they don't all have to be good. When you get ten, choose two or three to try first. If those ideas don't work, you have more to choose from.

Acknowledge Feelings

Third set of tools

Life will be more pleasant if you acknowledge feelings.

Feelings are not good nor bad.

Some people think of love as good and anger as bad. But it's not that simple. When love smothers a child and does not let her grow, that love is unhealthy. When anger is used to make good changes, that anger is healthy. For example, using anger to leave an abusive relationship is healthy.

Feelings and behavior are different from one another.

Feelings are inside you. Behavior is what you do with those feelings. Help children learn about feelings. Accept *their* feelings. Show them how you express your feelings in healthy ways. You can do these things by:

- Simple listening.
- Active listening.
- Granting in fantasy.

Simple Listening

Simple listening gives your child your attention. Use simple words to let them know you are listening. Use comments like: Uh-huh, okay, really? oh, yeah, hum, tell me more, etc.

When you simply listen, the child stays in charge of the problem. Sometimes they can solve it for themselves. For example:

Brian took my toy. *Oh.*
I wasn't done. *Hmm.*
He should have asked. *I see.*
I want it back. *Really?*
I'll ask him to give it back. *Okay.*

Active Listening

Children often feel angry or upset when they don't get their way. They need to learn to express feelings in a healthy way. You can help your child to accept his feelings by *active listening*.

Active listening focuses on feelings but does not try to change them.

Active listening involves: giving the child your full attention, describing the situation, and describing the child's feelings.

Give the child your full attention. Stop what you are doing. Go over to the child. Get down on eye level with the child. Use a gentle, caring voice to describe the feelings and situation you see.

Describe the situation. For example, *"Tommy knocked your blocks down." "You have to take a bath." "It is raining so we can't go to the park."*

Describe the child's feelings. Some feeling words are: frustrated, scared, angry, lonely, bored, disappointed, sad, or upset. Active listening accepts feelings. It does not judge them or criticize them.

You can fit the parts together in many different ways.

*"It's raining and we can't go to the park. You feel **disappointed**."*

*"You are **angry** that Emily knocked down your blocks."*

*"You're **scared** of the big dog."*　　　*"You miss your mommy and are **lonely** when she's gone."*

You can use active listening with happy feelings as well as with unhappy feelings. For example, *"You are proud of getting dressed all by yourself"* or *"You like dancing to that music."*

Active listening often feels funny at first. It gets easier with practice. Hang in there and keep trying.

Grant in Fantasy

Grant in fantasy gives the child in pretend what you can't give him or her in real life.

> Your child in the bathtub wants more troll dolls. Say, *"I wish I had one to give you. I wish I had a dozen for you. I wish I won the lottery and could buy **all** the trolls in town and dump them in the tub with you."*

When you acknowledge feelings, it is important to acknowledge pleasant feelings like happy, contented, and proud, as well as uncomfortable feelings like frustrated, angry, and scared.

Many parents feel confused about how to help their children deal with feelings. The section "Deal with Feelings" (page 27) shows how to use all the star points to help kids express feelings constructively.

19

Set Appropriate Limits

Fourth set of tools

Children need reasonable limits or rules.

Rules can be negotiable or non-negotiable. Negotiable rules are discussed in the chapter on power struggles (page 32).

Normal children test limits. Persistent children test limits many times. Remember that persistence is an excellent adult trait. You want to guide it, not crush it. Before you make a rule, decide what you will do if your child tests or challenges it.

State Clear Rules

Clear and appropriate rules are simple and geared to the child's age and personality.

Appropriate rules are *simple*. They use positive language. They tell the child what *to do* instead of what *not* to do. They make the child's choices clear. For example, *"no running inside,"* becomes *"walk inside."*

Appropriate rules are *geared to the child's age*. Although children differ, some behaviors are common at certain ages. To find out more about children's ages and stages, you can join a play group, babysit, take a class, or read a book.

✓ A *baby's* job is to learn to communicate and to trust people. When the baby cries, she is trying to tell you something.

✓ Soon the *young toddler* (6 to 18 months) can move around. He begins to explore the world. He chews things. He bangs things together. He drop things. He climbs in, under, and over things. He learns by trial and error. He needs to continue to trust that you will give him what he needs and to learn that he has choices.

✓ The *older toddler* (18 to 36 months) is beginning to think and feel for herself. She wants to do things by herself. She has tantrums. Language is coming, but it's not always easy.

✓ *Preschoolers* (3 to 5 years) are learning who they are. They are curious about the difference between male and female. They are trying different ways to be powerful. They need to learn to ask for what they want.

Appropriate limits are *suited to the child's personality*. There are several basic personality traits that do not change over time—*activity level* (active or still), *persistence* (keeps trying or gives up easily), *intensity of response* (loud or mild), and *mood* (pleasant or grumpy). If you have an active child, it's not reasonable to expect him to sit still in church or synagogue. If you have a child who laughs and cries loudly, don't take her where her noise will be a problem.

Develop Consequences

Children will test rules.

If you offer a child two yeses and she continues the unacceptable behavior, you may use a consequence.

A consequence is something that happens when she breaks the rule. Decide ahead of time what you will do if she ignores you again. Plan a consequence.

What is the difference between a threat and a consequence?

• **A threat** intends to frighten or shame a child into obedience rather than offer a real choice. It hurts or punishes, and lowers self-esteem. The tone of voice is critical and a threat may not be carried out.

• **A consequence** intends to guide or teach. The tone is calm and factual. It offers *true* choices and it will be carried out.

Four rules for a good consequence. A consequence is a real choice, is related to the child's behavior, is gently firm, and is something you will follow through with.

1. A consequence is **a real choice**. Both options are acceptable to the parent. For example, *"You can pick up your toys or I will put them away for a week."* The parent must be willing to put the toys away. If not, the statement is a threat.

2. The consequence is **related to the child's behavior.** There is a connection between the behavior and the consequence. For example, *"If you're not hungry enough for dinner, you're not hungry enough for dessert."* The connection is hunger. *"No dinner, no TV"* is not related.

3. A consequence is both **gentle** and **firm**. Your voice is pleasant and factual. For example, *"Do you want to put your coat on yourself or do you want me to do it?"* If your tone is mean, loud, or critical, the statement is a threat. With a consequence, your voice is calm and firm.

4. Finally, a consequence needs **follow through**. If your child refuses to choose, you must do what you said you would do. For example, *"Do you want to walk to bed or be carried?"* If she runs away, pick her up and say, *"I see you choose to be carried to bed."*

What can I use for consequences?

Lose a privilege
"You can drive the truck on the floor or play with something else."
▪ If he bangs it on the window, take the truck away. He loses the privilege of playing with the truck.

Do a kindness
"Watch where you are going or rebuild the tower of blocks."
▪ If Jess knocks down his sister's blocks, he must rebuild them and do something nice for her.

Re-do it
"Wash your hands well or do it over."
▪ If her hands are dirty for lunch, go with her to the sink and watch her do it right. Eventually she will find it is easier to do it right the first time.

Follow Through

To change your child's behavior, you *must* follow through.

If you tell your child to get off the table, you must take him off immediately if he does not get down. If you let him stay on the table, you are teaching him to ignore you.

The quicker you follow through, the quicker he will learn.

One parent reports—*"My sister counts to ten when she wants her kids to do something. I notice they move on nine! I count to three. My kids move at two."* You might give one reminder and then act.

Sometimes children test the same rule again and again. If you find yourself getting frustrated, try one of these tips.

Count
Count the number of times you put your child back in bed at night.

Pretend
Pretend you get five dollars every time you take her off the table. Plan what you would do with the money.

Call a friend
Ask your friend to tell you three things you do well.

Get relief
Get a babysitter, spouse, friend, or neighbor to give you a break.

If you are not going to enforce a rule, tell your child you have changed your mind. For example, *"I have changed my mind. You may jump on the sofa if you take your shoes off."* If you don't tell your children, they may assume you don't care about your other rules either.

Remember, you are a good person, even when your child is testing you.

Teach New Skills
Fifth set of tools

Some children have blind spots.

People expect them to have skills that they don't. They may need simple skills, like putting on clothes. Or, they may need complex skills, like remembering things or controlling their anger.

Tools you can use to teach new skills are:

- Modeling.
- Re-do it right.
- Shaping.

Modeling

Modeling is a powerful tool.

Young children are natural mimics. They try to do the things they see other people do—read, cook, shave.

Model exactly what you want your child to do. If you want your child to stop whining, you need to speak pleasantly. If you want your son to hang his coat up, then hang your coat up. If a young child doesn't see you hang your coat up, he may conclude that it magically happens like the sun rising and setting.

Modeling is useful, but children can't see what you are thinking. Give a short verbal explanation of your thoughts and actions.

Acknowledge the behavior you want. Encourage it with attention or praise. Otherwise it may disappear.

Children model your bad habits as well as your good ones. They may model anything they see or hear. If they see you smoking or eating in the living room, they will want to do it, too.

Re-do It Right

Re-do it right teaches physical habits.

To use re-do it right, return your child to the place where the error happened. Remind her of your expectations. And, assist the child to do it right if you need to. With this tool you must go *with* the child, *not tell* her to go.

> Your child forgot to close the front door. Walk over to her and say, *"Oops, you forgot to close the door."* Put your arm on her, turn her around, and walk back and close the door.

It usually takes children more time to re-do things than to do them right the first time, so most children learn quickly. It usually takes parents less time to teach this way than to *order* the child to do it.

Shaping

Shaping can be used for complicated behaviors.

Shaping divides the task into small steps and teaches the steps. You can teach by modeling or using simple instructions.

Three steps to teach a skill are:
- List what the child needs to learn.
- See what she can already do.
- Develop a plan and implement it.

List what abilities your child needs. Some jobs take physical skills. Some tasks need knowledge or information.

Zip a jacket	**Touch gently**
Concepts:	*Concepts:*
Understand words —	understand gentle *vs* rough
hold, tab, hole, in,	know when he is angry
pull, and up	know how to get attention
	know **how** to express anger
Physical skills:	(deep breaths)
Hand skills to —	
hold bottom of zipper	*Physical skills:*
insert tab in slot	breathing deeply (practice)
pull tab up	touching gently

Notice what the child can do. Can he sit still for something he wants? Can she understand needed words? Does she play with small things? Does he touch anything gently? Does he know how to "blow out mad feelings?"

Make a plan. First, teach the parts of the skill. Use modeling or simple instruction. Then put the pieces together. If your child has trouble, look for other skills needed or make smaller steps.

Deal with Feelings
Using all the points

Many people have trouble dealing with their children's feelings. You can use the five points we have talked about to help you.

Three things your child needs to know about feelings:

• *Feelings are different from actions.* When he feels mad, or scared, or happy, there are many ways he can express himself. For example, if a preschooler sees a dog he feels scared of he could stop in his tracks and freeze, run away crying, ask to be carried, or hum a happy tune and proceed. You may accept his feeling *and* put limits on the expression of his feeling.

• *Feelings are neither good nor bad.* Feelings are emotions. They give us information just like our eyes and ears. When you deny a feeling *("You're not scared of the nice doggie.")* or discount a feeling *("Forget it. It wasn't that bad."),* you teach children to mistrust their feelings.

• *Feelings change.* Children get so torn up about feelings because they live in the present moment. You can help them understand that feelings change by commenting on how your feelings change and their feelings change. For example, *"Remember how frustrated you were when your block tower fell down. You feel contented now."*

Teach New Skills

Have you ever felt something so strongly that you wanted to scream? Strong feelings have an energy that must go somewhere. A healthy thing to do is to use that energy to solve the problem. However, some people have trouble thinking clearly when their feelings are strong. They need ways to calm themselves down first.

Children need at least three different ways to calm themselves. The purpose is to reduce the energy level so they can think, not to eliminate the feeling. Here are several ways children can calm themselves:

✓ **Sound.** Tell someone how they feel. Sing a song. Listen to soothing music. Listen to marching music.

✓ **Movement.** Dance to music. Run around the block. Clean house or room. Shake out feelings.

✓ **Thoughts or pictures.** Imagine they're in a peaceful place. Blow out the bad feelings. Remember a time when they felt good. Draw a picture of how they feel now.

✓ **Plan to change the situation.** What can they do to make things better? They could talk to someone. Avoid the trouble.

✓ **Nurture themselves.** Take a warm bath. Read a book. Curl up in a rocking chair. Drink warm milk or apple juice.

✓ **Be creative.** Use the energy to paint, squish play dough, or pretend to be an animal. Draw what would help them feel better. Work in a garden. Build a sand castle.

How do I use these ideas? Offer your children ideas when they are calm. If you give them ideas when they feel already upset, it probably won't work. Here are three ways to start.

✓ Make it a game. *"Let's play a game called Dance Happy, Dance Mad. First let's dance like we are happy. Then we will dance like we are mad."*

"Remember the Dance game? You can get yourself calm by dancing mad and happy."

✓ Share your experience. *"Sometimes when I feel angry or scared, I make a happy place in my mind and go there. Tell me about a happy place you would like to go to when you are angry."*

"When you want to feel better, you can remember your happy place."

✓ Play pretend. *"Sometimes when people feel frustrated, it helps to run. Remember when you felt frustrated with the puzzle? Let's pretend you feel frustrated again and practice running."*
"Would you like to run and see if you feel calmer?"

Look for Good Behavior

When you teach a skill it is important to look for the new behavior. For example, if you want your daughter to take deep breaths when she feels frustrated rather than to cry, acknowledge her efforts.

You can praise or reward her effort. For example, *"You couldn't get the puzzle piece in and you took three breaths to calm yourself. Now you feel a little better."*

Acknowledge Feelings

Accepting your child's feelings helps your child feel loved and develop a feeling vocabulary.

Simple listening. Use comments like: Uh-huh, okay, really? oh, yeah, hum, tell me more, etc. For example:
Maggie was mean to me. *Oh.*
She hurt my feelings. *Hmm.*
She called me a klutz. *Really?*
I bumped her block tower. *I see.*
I'll apologize. *Okay.*

Active listening. Reflect back both the *feeling* and the *content* of the situation. *"Looks like you're frustrated you can't thread the needle."* Or, *"You're mad you can't go to school with your sister."*

29

Grant in fantasy Give children in pretend what you can't give them now. For example, your kids are tired of waiting at the airport for your plane home to be repaired. Mom says, *"Wouldn't it be fun if we had wings and didn't need to wait for the plane to go home? We could fly around rather than sit here and wait. You could fly to visit Grandma whenever you wanted. You could fly anywhere you wanted to visit."*

Avoid Problems

Sometimes parents try to avoid tantrums by giving the child what he or she wants. That may work in the short run; however, it is an unhealthy long-term solution. When you try to keep your children happy, you deny them the opportunity to learn to calm themselves.

One helpful way to reduce the intensity or frequency of tantrums is to reduce stress. You can reduce stress by allowing enough time for activities and regular exercise.

Physical exercise is most effective when children use big, continuous movements like running, climbing, tricycling, or dancing. Short arm movement like hitting may actually increase anger or frustration.

Allow enough time. When you continually push yourself and your child, the background stress level increases. Then when something happens, your child has less reserve to deal with the situation.

Set Limits

Although feelings are okay, some behavior is not acceptable. With feelings, as in other areas, children need clear rules, consequences, and follow through.

Clear rule. Acknowledge the feeling and clarify the limit. For example, *"It's okay to be mad at me, but you may not hit me. Find another way to tell me how mad you are."*

Consequences. Establish a consequence for misuse of feelings. *"If you hit me, I will put you down and step away."*

Follow through. Once you have established the rule and consequence, you must follow through kindly and consistently, even if you're tired. *"It's not okay to hit people. You have decided to be by yourself a bit."* Put the child down and move a few steps away. For a toddler, that "alone time" can be 15-20 seconds. For older children, more.

When you establish rules, make consequences, and follow through kindly, you are helping your child develop limits for himself.

Reduce
Power Struggles
Using all the tools

You can use the tools and processes we have talked about to deal with power struggles.

Both parents and children want their own way. The way you handle these struggles affects how many you have.

- If a child wins a conflict and the parent loses, conflicts happen over and over again.

- If the parent wins and the child loses, power conflicts *also* happen again and again.

Before you decide what to do, step back, and see where you are going.

Three questions to ask yourself about power conflicts:

- *What do I want my children to know about conflicts?* To feel helpless in power conflicts? To take what they want without regard to others? Or, to find solutions that work for everyone?

- *What is reasonable for my child now?* Some normal behavior is seen by parents as a power struggle. Toddlers explore their environment. Older toddlers say *"No"* and struggle to understand feelings. Preschoolers are curious about how people use power.

- *What is this conflict about?* Is this struggle the real issue or am I feeling angry or powerless about something else and using my child to bolster my self-esteem? Am I tired, stressed, or hungry?

We will see how each tool can be used to avoid or reduce power struggles.

Look for Good Behavior

Some children have a great need to be powerful.

Other children have a strong need for attention. Sometimes the only way they can get attention is with a power struggle.

Children can be powerful in many ways. You can help children by choosing your battles with care and finding ways for them to be powerful. It helps to praise kids when they cooperate.

✓ **Choose your battles with care.** It is not fun to fight with children over everything. Choose the issues that are important to you and let others go. For example, you might decide that *what* your child eats is more important than *how* she eats. Or you might decide that as long as your child sleeps, it doesn't matter where he sleeps.

✓ **Give kids power in some areas.** One way to give power is to offer children choices. For example, how much nutritious food to eat, what clothes to wear *(it rarely matters if the clothes match)*, which toy or book to take on a trip, or which story to read before taking a nap.

✓ **Let kids earn privileges.** Look at what your child wants and decide what *skill or abilities* she needs to earn that privilege. It is easier if the privilege is related to new behavior desired.

For example, Tracy wants to stay up late. She can *earn* the privilege of going to bed 30 minutes late on Saturday by going to bed pleasantly *(and on time)* other nights. Each time she goes to bed pleasantly Mom puts a star on the calendar. When Tracy has four stars, she can go to bed late on the next Saturday night.

Molly wants to hold the cat herself. She can earn the privilege by touching the cat gently when someone else holds him.

✓ **Praise cooperative behavior.** When your child cooperates with you, acknowledge that with praise. You could say, *"Thank you for coming so quickly."* Or *"Wow, you sure dressed fast."* Or, *"I appreciate the pleasant voice you used."*

Acknowledge Feelings

Acknowledging feelings decreases power struggles.

Acknowledging feelings tells your child, *"You're okay, even when I remain firm."* You can acknowledge feelings by active listening or offering skills to deal with feelings.

Active listening. You can see how *active listening* might work with three-year-old Tammy who wants a candy bar.

Tammy: I want it. I want it. I want it.
Dad: You're angry Mom won't let you have the candy bar.
Tammy: Yes! I want it, now!
Dad: You feel disappointed you have to wait until after lunch.
Tammy: Yeah.

Dealing with feelings. If she calmed a little but remained angry, Dad could offer her *tools to calm down.*

Dad: It seems like you're still pretty angry. Do you want to know what I do to calm down?
Tammy: (nods her head.)
Dad: There are three things. I take five deep breaths. That's one for each finger. Or, I go for a walk.
Tammy: What else?
Dad: I imagine the angry feelings draining down my legs, into my feet, out my toes, and dribbling on the ground.
Tammy: That's silly.
Dad: Yes. And it helps me. What would you like to do?
Tammy: Let's go for a walk.

In both stories, Dad accepted Tammy's feelings. This acceptance reduced the power struggle.

Avoid Problems

You can reduce power struggles by changing the situation, reducing stress, and offering two yeses.

Change the situation by side-stepping it, using simple distractions, or doing the unexpected.

• *Side-step.* If your four-year-old wants a new pair of shoes every time you pass a shoe shop—don't walk by the shoe shop. That way you avoid the battle. If you can't avoid the shoe shop, tell your child an interesting story so she will look at you, not at the store.

• *Simple distraction.* Most toddlers are easy to distract. Simply give the child something new or interesting to listen to or to do. She will usually stop what she is doing. However, somewhere between 1½ and 2½ years old simple distraction fails to work as well.

• *Do something unexpected.* When you have the same conflict again and again, you can often stop it by doing something unexpected. The unexpected can be something silly or it can be the opposite of what you feel like doing. For example, if you want to yell, go up to your daughter and whisper in her ear.

Reduce stress. Regular exercise can help you relax and avoid conflicts with your child. Exercise is best when it has long smooth motions like walking, running, or swimming. Short movements, like hitting or punching, can make you more tense.

Give two yeses. Telling the child what she may do often avoids a power struggle. For example, if your child does not want to leave a friend's house, you could say, *"It's time to go and you want to stay. You may invite Tommy over tomorrow or call him on the phone when we get home."* Both of these ideas honor the child's desire to be with her friend.

Set Limits

Parents frequently get into power struggles with children over limits.

Negotiable and non-negotiable limits. Children need both non-negotiable rules and negotiable ones. Non-negotiable limits teach obedience. Negotiable rules teach responsibility.

Non-negotiable rules are needed for safety and moral issues: wear a seat belt, hold my hand crossing the street, walk with scissors, touch people gently.

Negotiable rules teach children to think about the situations and act responsibly. Negotiable rules have another benefit; they encourage cooperation. Either children or parents can start negotiations for negotiable rules.

Non-negotiable rule	*Negotiable rule*
Bedtime 7 P.M., always.	Bedtime 7 P.M. except on special occasions, like holidays.
No food in the living room.	Eating in the living room is okay with permission.
Leave the figurines alone. (Don't touch.)	If you want to touch the figurines, ask me to hold them for you.
Draw *only* on scratch paper.	Ask me if you want to draw on something else.

A Better Way is a simple form of negotiation. You can use A Better Way to reduce power struggles. It invites cooperation rather than conflict. You can see how the parent negotiates in the example below.

Dad's way — Son goes to bed now (7:00 P.M.).
Child's way — He goes to bed *late*.
A Better Way — Son goes to bed at 7:10 P.M.

This bedtime is later than Dad would like. It is earlier than the child would like. But it is *workable* for both.

A Better Way works best when the child comes up with the idea. The parent describes the positions. Then the parent asks the child for ideas. Often the child's ideas are workable. If not, explain what is wrong and suggest the closest idea to the child's you can think of.

For the first two or three times you use this tool, use the child's idea unless it is unsafe or very impractical. Once the child knows how it works, you can work together more.

Before you use A Better Way you need to explain the idea to your children. To explain A Better Way you can:
- Use puppets to act out the following story.
- Make up your own story using a stuffed animal or toy figures.
- Recall a problem you had, and talk about what a better way to solve it would have been.

When you use A Better Way remind children that:

✓ The better way will be *different* from either of the ideas you start with. And,

✓ There are ideas that will work for both of you. All you have to do is find them.

A Better Way is a fun way to end power struggles. You can see how it worked below. Mom wanted to give Lori a bath now:

Lori: No bath. No bath. No bath. (3-year-old with 7-year-old brother Kevin nearby)

Mom: My way is—I give you a bath now. Your way is—I give you a bath after breakfast. What is a better way?

Lori: Kevin do it!

Mom: Kevin, will you give Lori a bath?

Kevin: What do I have to do?

Mom: Lori, what does he need to do?

Lori: Run the bath water.

Mom: Kevin, is that okay with you?

Kevin: (Nods and goes to the bathroom)

Mom: Well done, Lori. You found a better way.

Teach New Skills

Look at what you want your child to know about power struggles. Does your child have the skills needed for conflict resolution? If not, you can teach the skills.

Modeling. Verbally describe your thought process to your child. For example: *"The kids are noisy and I need some quiet. What can I do? Take them for a walk. Ask them to be quiet. Read them a story. Put on a headset and listen to soothing music. What will I try first? I will listen to soothing music. If that doesn't work, I'll take them for a walk."*

Shaping. Divide the task into small pieces and then teach those pieces. For example, for conflict resolution you need the ability to (1) differentiate between what children want and what they need, (2) state their needs clearly, (3) listen to other's needs, and (4) negotiate. Each of these skills can be introduced separately. You can get ideas in the book *Kids Can Cooperate* by Elizabeth Crary.

These five sets of tools can be used for any problem you have. The next chapter shows you how.

Solving Problems with the Tools

You can use the fifteen tools to solve any problems you face. You can use the tools randomly for annoying problems. However, if the problem is serious or very frustrating, use the following process to plan your approach.

Sometimes you can stop what you are doing with your child and think the problem through. Other times, you can get through the moment of crisis and then work on the problem before it happens again.

Four-Step Process

Stop and focus. If you are in the middle of a crisis, calm yourself enough so you can think.
✓ What does the child *do* or *say* that is a problem? How frequently does this happen?
✓ Decide specifically what you want the child *to do* instead.
✓ Is the desired behavior realistic for the child's age and temperament?

Think of ideas. Usually when people list ideas they write what they already know. Brainstorming *begins* after that point.
✓ List lots of ideas. Aim for ten ideas.
✓ List different ideas. Use the star points to come up with new ideas.
✓ Some ideas can be silly. When your mind is free enough for silly ideas, it's free enough to think of new good ideas.

Act effectively. Review your ideas and choose one that you think will work for you and your child.
✓ Get the support you need to carry off the plan.

✓ Follow through. The most wonderful plan will not work if you don't "do it."

Review, revise, reward. Few plans work well the first time.
✓ Schedule a time to review your progress.
✓ Revise your plan. Most successful parents need to tweak the plan several times before the situation is satisfactorily resolved.
✓ Reward yourself. Reward your success or your effort.

Sample Problem

Here's a sample problem to show you how.

Stop and focus

■ *Describe the problem.*
　　Be specific.
　　What does the child say or
　　　do that is a problem?

My child whines or cries if she doesn't get what she wants. This time she wanted my new lipstick.

■ *Gather information.*
　　How often does it happen?
　　When does it happen?
　　Is the behavior common
　　　for the child's age?

She cries about half the time. It often happens when she is tired. I see other kids have tantrums, too.

■ *Decide what you want.*
　　Be specific.
　　What do you want your
　　　child *to do*? (Instead of
　　　not do.)

I want her to find another way to let me know she is unhappy. She can pout (that's better than crying) or talk with a calm voice.

Think of ideas

　　List as many ideas as you can.
　　Try to find two for each
　　　category.

Some ideas I can try are:

■ *Look for good behavior.*
　　Give attention
　　Praise
　　Reward

Give attention. Look at her while I listen.
Praise. Say, "Thank you for speaking pleasantly."
Reward. Tell her we will go to the park if she speaks pleasantly all afternoon.

- *Avoid problems.*
  Make expectations clear
  Give two yeses
  Change things

- *Set reasonable limits.*
  Clear rules
  Consequences
  Follow through

- *Acknowledge feelings.*
  Simple listening
  Active listening
  Grant in fantasy

- *Teach new skills.*
  Modeling
  Shaping
  Re-do it right

Two yeses. Say, *"I will put a dot of my new lipstick where you want."* Or, *"You may use my old lipstick or chapstick."*
Change things. Keep things that I don't want to share out of sight.

Clear rule. Speak pleasantly or the answer is *"No."*
Follow through. If she cries, walk away. If she talks, listen.

Active listening. Say, *"You're disappointed that I won't let you use my lipstick."*
Grant in fantasy. *"Wouldn't it be fun to have a magic genie to help you do whatever you wanted?"*

Re-do it right. Remind her to ask pleasantly. When she asks pleasantly, offer to put a little lipstick on her.

Act effectively

- *Look at your ideas.*
  What will work best for you? What will work for your child?
- *Choose an idea.*
- *Make a plan.*

Choose an idea. I will offer her a choice of my old lipstick or chapstick.
Make a plan. If she cries, I will turn on the music so her crying doesn't bother me.

Review, revise, reward

- *Review your plan.*
- *Change it, if needed.*
- *Reward yourself* for success or effort.

Change, if needed. If this doesn't work, I can try active listening or a reward.
Reward myself. When I have followed through three days, I will meet a friend for coffee.

Now you can try your plan.

Your Work Sheet

Stop and focus

- *Describe the problem.*
  Be specific.
  What does the child say or
    do that is a problem?

- *Gather information.*
  How often does it happen?
  When does it happen?
  Is the behavior common for
    the child's age?

- *Decide what you want.*
  Be specific.
  What do you want your child
    to do? (Instead of not do)

Think of ideas

List as many ideas as you can.
Try to find two for each
  category.

- *Look for good behavior.*
    Give attention
    Praise
    Reward

- *Avoid problems.*
    Make expectations clear
    Give two yeses for each no
    Change the situation

- *Set appropriate limits.*
  State clear rules
  Develop consequences
  Follow through
  A Better Way

- *Acknowledge feelings.*
  Simple listening
  Active listening
  Grant in fantasy

- *Teach new skills.*
  Modeling
  Shaping
  Re-do it right

Act effectively

- *Look at your ideas.*
  What will work best for
  you? What will work best
  for your child?
- *Choose an idea.*
- *Make a plan.*

Review, revise, reward

- *Review your plan.*
- *Revise, if needed.*
- *Congratulate yourself!*

Where to Go Next

Parenting is easier when you have a variety of ideas.

Ten or more ideas work best. When you get the hang of it, you will be able to come up with 20 or 25. Remember, they don't all have to be good ideas.

When you begin to list ideas, you will start with ones you already know. Usually they are ideas that have not worked, so you need *more* ideas. Four ways to get ideas are:
- Use books.
- Ask people for ideas.
- Pretend.
- Take a class.

Use Books

Here are several useful books. You can borrow books from the library, a friend, or buy them at a book store. A book store can order them for you if the books are out of stock.

■ *Love & Limits.* Look through the examples for each set of tools and see how you can adapt them for your problem.

■ *Tools for Everyday Parenting Series: 365 Wacky, Wonderful Ways to Get Your Child to Do What You Want* by Elizabeth Crary. Seattle: Parenting Press, 1994.

■ *Without Spanking or Spoiling: A Practical Approach to Toddler and Preschool Guidance,* Second Edition, by Elizabeth Crary. Seattle: Parenting Press, 1993. Offers more tools you can use.

■ *Help! for Parents of Children from Birth to Five: Tried and True Solutions to Parents' Everyday Problems* by Jean I. Clarke. San Francisco: Harper, 1993.

■ *Help! for Parents of School-aged Children and Teenagers: Tried and True Solutions to Parents' Everyday Problems* by Jean I. Clarke. San Francisco: Harper, 1993.

■ *Child Behavior* by Frances L. Ilg *et al.* New York: HarperCollins, 1992. Talks about what children are like at different ages.

Ask People for Ideas

Ask five people for two ideas each. Say, *"I'm collecting ideas. What are two things I could do when my child. . . ."*

✓ **Call friends.** If they have children too, you could let them read this book and work together using the tools in this book.

✓ **Ask relatives.** If you have a sister, aunt, dad, or someone you think is good with children, ask him or her for ideas to handle the problem.

✓ **Ask your pastor, priest, or rabbi.** Most clergy are trained to help families.

✓ **Ask a social worker.** She may have some ideas. If not, she should be able to find someone else to help you.

Pretend!

Being silly can relax you enough to think of new ideas. Pretend you are:
    — the president. How would he or she handle this?
    — a magician. How could magic help?
    — rich. How could money help?
    — from outer space. What could you do then?
    — the wisest person you know. What might she do?
Take these ideas and adapt them. If you need help, ask friends or professionals to help you.

Take a Class

Many community groups now offer parenting classes. Some ideas are:

- community colleges
- churches
- YMCA's or YWCA's
- childbirth education groups
- family service agencies
- hospitals
- public schools

You can look up numbers for these groups in the phone book. Call and ask for information. Or you could ask a friend or social worker for more information.

What's Holding You Back?

If you have been through these ideas and still have problems, here are three things you can do.

1. **Hunt for *poor* ideas.**

   Sometimes people have trouble finding ideas because they want *perfect* ideas. One way to get past that is to list poor ideas first. Write down all the bad ideas you know. Sometimes, that will free your brain up to think of good ideas.

2. **Take care of yourself.**

   Sometimes people have good ideas, but can't make them work. When that happens, parents need to find out why. Maybe you are doing too much. Maybe your growing up was difficult and you're trying to give your child what you wished you'd had. Whatever the reason, take care of yourself so you can take care of your children.

3. Get help.

Sometimes people get stuck, and they need some help. Talk to a doctor, counselor, minister, social worker, relative, or friend. Ask them to help you find the help you need. You can also call your local crisis number. They can find someone to help you.

Congratulations!

You made it through this book. That took planning and persistence. With those skills you can solve your problems.

Remember, the more ideas the better. Stick with the idea you choose long enough to give it a fair trial. You don't have to be successful the first time you try something. Or the second time you try. Or the third time you try. Keep trying until something works.

Love & Limits has given you lots of information. Store what you don't need now for use in the future. You can take the time you need to make this STAR approach work for you.

Have fun!

More Guidance Tools for Creative Parenting

Skill-building books for children and parents that promote peace in your family, from Parenting Press, Inc.

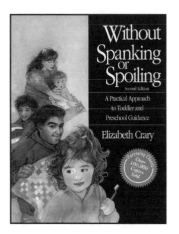

Without Spanking or Spoiling, 2nd ed., by Elizabeth Crary gives parents four major parenting approaches. Parents can choose a guidance method that best fits their child's temperament. Includes a problem-solving process and 150 ideas to solve ten common behavior problems. Useful with 1-5 years. 128 pages, $14.95 paper, $19.95 library

Help! The Kids Are at It Again: Using Kids' Quarrels to Teach "People" Skills, by Elizabeth Crary offers tools to solve a common family problem–sibling fights. Useful with all ages. *Family Channel Seal of Quality* award winner. 96 pages, $11.95 paper, $18.95 library

Pick Up Your Socks . . . and Other Skills Growing Children Need!, by Elizabeth Crary and illustrated by Pati Casebolt, shows parents how to teach responsibility to children. Useful with 3-12 years. 112 pages, $14.95 paper, $19.95 library

---